First World War
and Army of Occupation
War Diary
France, Belgium and Germany

60 DIVISION
Headquarters, Branches and Services
Royal Army Medical Corps
Assistant Director Medical Services
1 November 1915 - 31 December 1915

WO95/3026/7

The Naval & Military Press Ltd
www.nmarchive.com
Published in association with The National Archives

Published by

The Naval & Military Press Ltd

Unit 10 Ridgewood Industrial Park,

Uckfield, East Sussex,

TN22 5QE England

Tel: +44 (0) 1825 749494

www.naval-military-press.com

www.nmarchive.com

This diary has been reprinted in facsimile from the original. Any imperfections are inevitably reproduced and the quality may fall short of modern type and cartographic standards.

© **Crown Copyright**
Images reproduced by permission of The National Archives, London, England, 2015.

Contents

Document type	Place/Title	Date From	Date To
Heading	WO95/3026/7		
Miscellaneous	War Diary	03/09/1915	03/09/1915
Miscellaneous	War Diary	05/10/1915	05/10/1915
War Diary	Bishops Stortford	01/11/1915	29/11/1915
Heading	War Diary of the A.D.M.S.60th (London) Division From 1st December 1915 To 31st December 1915 Volume 2		
War Diary	Bishops Stortford	01/12/1915	31/12/1915

WO 95/3026/7

WAR DIARY.

2/4th London Field Ambulance)
)
2/4th London Field Ambulance)   60th (London) Division.
)
2/6th London Field Ambulance)

WAR STATION.
2/4th London Field Ambulance - Saffron Walden
2/5th London Field Ambulance - Hatfield Broad Oak.
2/6th London Field Ambulance - Bishop's Stortford.

PERIOD.

AUGUST 1915.

TRAINING.

Progressing slowly, and now much hampered by influx of recruits and want of officers.

DISCIPLINE.

Very good.   Much improved on going under canvas.

ADMINISTRATION.

Good.

EQUIPMENT.

Want of wagons still render Field ambulances absolutely immobile in the event of an order to move.

PREPARATION FOR IMPERIAL SERVICE.

As given above, the shortage of Officers is a most serious stoppage.   In the 3 Field Ambulances alone this Division is 16 Medical Officers short.

Colonel
Assistant Director of
Medical Services
60th London Division

3.9.15

WAR DIARY.

2/4th London Field Ambulance)
2/4th London Field Ambulance) 60th (London) Division.
2/6th London Field Ambulance)

WAR STATION.

2/4th London Field Ambulance - Saffron Walden.
2/5th London Field Ambulance - Hatfield Broad Oak.
2/6th London Field Ambulance - Bishop's Stortford.

PERIOD.

AUGUST 1915.

TRAINING.

Progressing slowly, and now much hampered by influx of recruits and want of officers.

DISCIPLINE.

Very good. Much improved on going under canvas.

ADMINISTRATION.

Good.

EQUIPMENT.

Want of wagons still render Field ambulances absolutely immobile in the event of an order to move.

PREPARATION FOR IMPERIAL SERVICE.

As given above, the shortage of Officers is a most serious stoppage. In the 3 Field Ambulances alone this Division is 16 Medical Officers short.

signature
Colonel
Assistant Director of
Medical Services
60th London Division

3.9.15

WAR DIARY.

2/4th London Field Ambulance)
2/4th London Field Ambulance) 60th (London) Division.
2/6th London Field Ambulance)

WAR STATION.
2/4th London Field Ambulance - Saffron Walden.
2/5th London Field Ambulance - Hatfield Broad Oak.
2/6th London Field Ambulance - Bishop's Stortford.

PERIOD.

AUGUST 1915.

TRAINING.

Progressing slowly, and now much hampered by influx of recruits and want of officers.

DISCIPLINE.

Very good. Much improved on going under canvas.

ADMINISTRATION.

Good.

EQUIPMENT.

Want of wagons still render Field ambulances absolutely immobile in the event of an order to move.

PREPARATION FOR IMPERIAL SERVICE.

As given above, the shortage of Officers is a most serious stoppage. In the 3 Field Ambulances alone this Division is 16 Medical Officers short.

Bodwick
Colonel
Assistant Director of
Medical Services
2nd London Division

3.9.15

WAR DIARY.

2/4th Field Ambulance)
2/5th Field Ambulance) 60th (London) Division.
2/6th Field Ambulance)

WAR STATIONS.

2/4th Field Ambulance - Saffron Walden.
2/5th Field Ambulance - Hatfield Broad Oak
2/6th Field Ambulance - Bishop's Stortford.

PERIOD.

SEPTEMBER 1915.

TRAINING.

Much improved during past month, especially in the 2/6th London Field Ambulance, who have been entirely relieved of the Reception Hospital which was taken over by the 60th (London) Casualty Clearing Station. The 2/6th London Field Ambulance was thus able to work entirely at Field exercises.

DISCIPLINE.

Very good. High standard still kept up under canvas.

ADMINISTRATION.

Good under circumstances, but very much hampered by shortage of Medical Officers.

EQUIPMENT.

Harness and Wagons are the greatest deficiency.

The present type of wagon (Studebaker) issued to Field Ambulances is _absolutely_ useless for the purpose.

[signature]
Colonel.
A.D.M.S. 60th (London) Division.

Bishop's Stortford.
OCTOBER 5th 1915.

WAR DIARY or **INTELLIGENCE SUMMARY.**

Army Form C. 2118.

A.D.M.S. 60th (London) Division

NOVEMBER

Place	Date	Hour	Summary of Events and Information	Remarks and references to Appendices
Bisht, Saffron	Nov 1st		Issued instructions to all concerned re Influenza & East Anglian Casualty Hearing Clerks now being from Hertford Village & Cambridge	(E.A. 3703, 3706) (E.A.D.)
			Made application for Equipment of J.D. Reidit & Matron Cma Clearing Hosp. York	(E.A. 3707) (E.A.D.)
	2nd		Inspected Wrexham Nat. Mil. Hosp. & taken over Reception Hospital there but Recruits arriving. Satisfactory	(E.A.D.)
			Inspected Casualty Clearing Station Hospital & York (Park Hosp.) Camp. — Getting very	
			cold & uncomfortable. Important to have it once if possible.	(E.A.D.)
	3rd		Made application through B.G. (Remounts) Command to G.O.C. Wrexham Nat.	(E.A. 3717) (E.A.D.)
			On application from A.D.M.S. 2/1 Mtd Div. (as others & Lond. Londn Yeo. Yeomtry)	
			Cav Regts & Div'l Mobile Column	(E.A. 3721)
			Attendance of J.D. Cantwell & 2/Lieut. Offcl	(E.A. 3725).
	4th		Issued General Instructions to all ranks on treatment of Scabies & Pediculosis Capitis	(E.A. 3729, 3731)
			and made call units to take further steps for treatment	(E.A. 3735)
			Recvt RCS orders re Influenza for Double Treatment	(E.A. 3736) (E.A.D.)
	6th		On application from A.D.M.S. 2/1 Lond. Bde. (not others & Lond. Divn. Yeo. Cavalry)	
			Cav Regts & Urban B. Chilern	(E.A. 3739) (E.A.D.)

WAR DIARY
or
INTELLIGENCE SUMMARY.

Army Form C. 2118.

(Erase heading not required.)

Place	Date	Hour	Summary of Events and Information	Remarks and references to Appendices
B.H.Qs. (Chittagong)	Nov 8.		Forwarded application of A.D.M.S. 3rd Divn., that Quarter Master Lt Greenhoud of RAMC Commission to 3rd Jon Medical Details 2nd Ambulance.	(md)
	9		Appointment of Lt Falkener Junr. v/ lt M.S. Cooper A.S.C. at Lithology (E.R. 3764) Alterations for Court Martial on OSergt Stuttham from OC 2/3 Middlesex Regt — forwarded to Brigade. (E.R. 3767)	(md)
	10		Inspected new transport of 2/4th Field Ambulance. Men well turned out & transport in first rate order. Well conducted. Transport horses not enough to take ___.	(md)
			Received from G.O.C. L. Suffolk Welfare to report O.O. & Court Martial of Shot ? 188th Brigade.	(md)
	11		Accompanied G.O.C. to ____ in Street ____ & Entanglements & Schools of 181st Brigade.	(md)
			Go-holloy had gL____ first up the Elmsham Hall. Read urgent _____ to Road Convertor. Held the _____ was extremely _____ or nothing ____ (F.R. 3802) (md)	(md)
	12		Received Order to all units & circulate____ info for ham Decoro of Gibeck (E.R. 3815.)	(md)

Army Form C. 2118.

WAR DIARY
or
INTELLIGENCE SUMMARY.
(Erase heading not required.)

Instructions regarding War Diaries and Intelligence Summaries are contained in F. S. Regs., Part II. and the Staff Manual respectively. Title pages will be prepared in manuscript.

Place	Date	Hour	Summary of Events and Information	Remarks and references to Appendices
Belfast Stafford	Nov 12th		Appointment of D.C. of Hertford & Clerk of 2 Med. Matron at Hertford. (E.A. 3817.) Visited in Hertford and conversed with Major Felt & Edward Hall, &	
	13th		Carfried British Oatford. (E.A. 3815) Visited in Hertford & Hostelin of Cuerselfland hospitals at Halifax Road Oak. (E.A. 3830)	(F3) (F4)
	15th		Inspected Western Receptian Hospital & 2/1st 2nd Durham at "Carfuis" Britots Ostend.	(F5)
	16th		Visited others & all medical officers at hospitals will be kept during a change of Rank. (E.A. 3841) Beside a/1 & keeping a diary of same. Inspected Receptian Hospitals & 2/5 & 2/90 Cumberlands at Westport. Main Hospitals 5000, but the work been for scale body. (See Sheet Other as Smith attention to this.	(F6) (F7)
	17th		Received telegram for A.D.M.S. 3rd Army re Capt. Munro's conduct at Redeic Hav John Walker calling for report, arrest & Court Enter force. "Sent Wire to O.C. 180th Fd Ord. & Proc Linton out of bounds Sent sanitary officer to investigate & report	(F8) (F9) (F10)

Army Form C. 2118.

WAR DIARY
or
INTELLIGENCE SUMMARY.
(Erase heading not required.)

Instructions regarding War Diaries and Intelligence Summaries are contained in F. S. Regs., Part II. and the Staff Manual respectively. Title pages will be prepared in manuscript.

Place	Date	Hour	Summary of Events and Information	Remarks and references to Appendices
Aldsh. Newport	Mar 17th		Forwarded report on Sanitn. Arrand. of H.Q. Central Force & Coy. of A.D.M.S. of Army for Dir. Gurne orders. Sale M.O. & asst. Sanity. Dept. i/c Mil. (CA. 3882.)	(A.)
			Inspected Infection Reception Hospital, Carpairs. Hookum Road. Repairs nearly complete.	(B.)
			Visits Disinfecting Station & Isolation Hospital & Workhouse. All well.	(C.)
	18th		Continued.	
			Read D.A.D.M.S. & Inspect chapel of 2/16:17 yeh R.F.A. & 1/1st Mid. Middlesex Inspected Men & Transport of 2/5:4th Battn. Buckhams Pt. Newport. Men all look turned out, & examined & First Aid in in b (men). Newport turned out, (feet). as b f/ken f/r Troops	(D.)
	19th		Whole of Division 1671 officers Medically examined as b f/ken f/r Troops.	(E.)
			Orders.	
	20th		Visit by Sanitary Officer, Central Force. to inspect ADMS of Division. Inspected A.D.M.S. of A. C. & H.Q. Staff & Sanitary Officer, accompanied by Divisional Sanitary Officer.	
	23rd		Recived instructions from C.S.M. Laboratory, Cambridge, that P6. Stilwell 17/2/22 Battn. + Pt. Jones, R. 2/1st 16 Battn had suffered from Cerebro Spinal Fever. Gave Orders to O.C. 2/14 + 2/1 Crush to Open men fell the infective "Carriers".	(F.)

1577 Wt. W10791/1773 500,000 1/15 D. D. & L. A.D.S.S./Forms/C. 2118.

WAR DIARY
or
INTELLIGENCE SUMMARY.
(Erase heading not required.)

Army Form C. 2118.

Instructions regarding War Diaries and Intelligence Summaries are contained in F. S. Regs., Part II. and the Staff Manual respectively. Title pages will be prepared in manuscript.

Place	Date	Hour	Summary of Events and Information	Remarks and references to Appendices
	24th		To Amara then over to N Eastern General Hospital for treatment. Two "Contacts" of 2/1st Batt. with C.S.M., one for Helfeld Report sent. See also Damaged 5/1st Gen. Genene Hospital Come Org. See therapist Army Form "Inspection".	(E.B. 3940)
			Ref pneld 2/6th Field Ambulance at Mambré. Transport excellent. Warned Capt. Hanks at present attached 5 7/13 N° Nats that the sent of 2/15th & 2/15th Nat should have & there to Hartford, it cannot be transferred to there et c: received orders. Jell there lives.	(E.B.)
	25th		Inspected the 58th London Casualty Clearing Station at Chouain N.G. General Turnout excellent. First Aid — Very Poor. Hospital — Very well kept.	(E.B.)
			Test turn of O.C. Genl. G. to export Vent records for the blue facilities for Reception Hospital of Field Ambulances. & reports.	(E.B.)
	27th		Given & report to walk with 3rd Army. (E.B. 3962)	(E.B.)
			Received report from O.C. Casualty Clearing Station Not Likely LtKelly / Royal Highn Corps	

WAR DIARY
or
INTELLIGENCE SUMMARY.
(Erase heading not required.)

Army Form C. 2118.

Place	Date	Hour	Summary of Events and Information	Remarks and references to Appendices
	28th		Rate fallen will be desirable at Standen at 5.15 p.m. 28th inst & MN/Ala Cornwall Class Station but felt this then to M.K.Ambulance of Crospool turn to 16 Ridings Stratford Ave Helpuke. I visited 16 patient today at 12 noon afterwards field 2/year of Medl Corps (Ens. 3980.) Particulars various cunt, he, & certain helped but wind hot, & Med inde Rack, SM.) Visited Manor ho h to ascertain if suitable for billing a Retention Intervened police, Remit emergency & Centium doors, also Billing Offices (2/25/Phh, Found plans Purple Furlock & Dexist Came Others quarter. (ER. 6002.) Repairs almost complete. ERS. Inspected "Carparen" Reception Hospital (infection).	
	29th			

E. B. Jowers
COLONEL
ASSISTANT DIRECTOR OF
MEDICAL SERVICES
60TH (LONDON) DIVISION.

1. XII. 15.

C O N F I D E N T I A L.

WAR DIARY of the

A.D.M.S.60th (LONDON) DIVISION.

From 1st DECEMBER 1915 to 31st DECEMBER 1915.

VOLUME 2. (5 pages).

Army Form C. 2118.

WAR DIARY
or
INTELLIGENCE SUMMARY.
(Erase heading not required.)

WAR DIARY of A.D.M.S. 60th (2nd) Yeos. in DECEMBER. Pg 1.

Instructions regarding War Diaries and Intelligence Summaries are contained in F. S. Regs., Part II. and the Staff Manual respectively. Title pages will be prepared in manuscript.

Place	Date	Hour	Summary of Events and Information	Remarks and references to Appendices
BISHOPS STORTFORD	1.12.15		Visit to HAVERHILL and view & occupy Mil: civilian Medical Practitioners & Col & M.O. & 2/20th Batt: when i/ Matrons. St Goodman consulted Pact: Made all arrangements with him re transfer of sick &c.	(No.)
"	3.12.15		Got phone message from A.D.M.S. 3rd Army, that A.D.M.S. 3rd Army at ELSENHAM HALL v. informed Same. Received application that ELSENHAM HALL Recn for Hospital might be taken over as a Civilian Hospital. Forwarded to 3rd Army (F.R. 6032) Sent report to O.C. A.S.C. Mail at Maller Car & Drivers & Field Ambulances on Medical Sick Carb: me to duty within for pumpm. (E.A. 6043)	(No.) (No.) (No.) (No.)
"	4.12.15 6.12.15		Instructed M.O. 2/14th Batt: to visit Debenture barracks, BRAINTREE Daily. Received Instruction from A.D.M.S. 3rd Army & Division Captain medicine Practitioners at R.C. at BISHOPS STORTFORD & LITTLEBURY & put 1/4th 2nd Amb & 6th Class at former v M.D. 1/18 & Natt: at latter (F.R. 6072)	(No.) (No.)
"	8.12.15		Received orders for A.D.M.S. 3rd Army & details 2 both Ambulances & the 7th Y. 8th Provinsional Brigades.	(No.)

Army Form C. 2118.

WAR DIARY
INTELLIGENCE SUMMARY
(Erase heading not required.)

Page 2

Place	Date	Hour	Summary of Events and Information	Remarks and references to Appendices
BISHOPS STORTFORD	8.12.15		Accompanied G.O.C. at Inspection of ELSENHAM HALL Hospital.	875.
"	9.12.15		A.D.M.S. 3rd Army Inspected "CANFIELD" Inspection Hospital & 2/4th & 2/2nd East & 2/2nd West. Notified that application for "Cold & influenza" & "Hand of Salmon" for 60 patients & 9 of the Cavalry Casualty Clearing Station Hospital. Prepared 2/5 3rd Amb. Recep tion Hosp. for the NEWPORT. Cooking arrangements Lot (?) – (?) – (New inspection of same. Also inspector R.M. Stone.	878. 878. 878. 879.
"	10.12.15		Attended lecture on "Gas attacks & the Uses of Combating" at R.A.M. College Millbank. Applied for 1 doz "Gas Helmets" for instructional purposes & Major Chisholm Millbank 6830.	879.
"	11.12.15		Inspected Disinfecting Station & 2/2 Lond. Sanitary Co. Suffolk Walden. Wrote suggestion for Improvement of Disinfector.	C.A.D.
"	13.12.15		Received memo from Rear Branch re Clothing 64 Inf: Bn of same F. issued orders & all units concerning same (E.A. 61 U.S.)	879.
"	14.12.15		Received notification from A.D.M.S. 3/3 Lond. Dist. that Col. Petablic would replace it Mornay as Sanitary Officer. Until agreed that be complete permanently attached.	880.

Army Form C. 2118.

WAR DIARY
or
INTELLIGENCE SUMMARY.
(Erase heading not required.)

Instructions regarding War Diaries and Intelligence Summaries are contained in F. S. Regs., Part II. and the Staff Manual respectively. Title pages will be prepared in manuscript.

Page 3

Place	Date	Hour	Summary of Events and Information	Remarks and references to Appendices
BISHOP STORTFORD	15.12.15		Divisional Sanitary Officer accompanied A.D.M.S. 3rd Army to CHICHESTER Hospital Camp. "Oakleighton" examined. 3rd Army Hut, as Major Miller (D.A.D.M.S.) had been found medically unfit for overseas, to-night be attached to 3rd Army H.Q. as M.O.	(A)
	16.12.15		Again reattached by G.O.C. Local Government Board Sanitary Inspector, to visit Sewage arrangements at...	(B)
	17.12.15		EBERNHAM HALL: Satisfact. Lieut Tebb's arrival at Station as Sanitary Officer at 3rd Army H.Q.	
	18.12.15		Major Miller (D.A.D.M.S.) left for duty at 3rd Army H.Q. Notification of Diphtheria outbreak at GOSSFIELD. Requested N.O.K. 180th and 7th Brigade putting GOSSFIELD out of bounds.	(C) (D)
	19.12.15		Report from O.C. Sanitary Section. SAFFRON WALDEN that every house in country by numerous condition. Velocio very dirty. Forwarded copy to H.Q. that this expansion action ought to be taken. Made arrangements for two "Thresh" Disinfectors at NEWPORT to be transferred to SAFFRON WALDEN, in exchange for two Small Pox Disinfectors.	(E) (F)

1577 Wt.W10791/1773 500,000 1/15 D.D.&L. A.D.S.S./Forms/C. 2118.

WAR DIARY

INTELLIGENCE SUMMARY

Army Form C. 2118.

Page 4

Place	Date	Hour	Summary of Events and Information	Remarks and references to Appendices
19SMPS STRATFORD	20th/12/15		Received Memo from A.D.M.S. 3rd Army asking for population re centre of Op[?]Mahini. Work etc carried out.	(M)
"	22nd/12/15		Asked H.Q. for authority of purchase Breakalls for use of Sanitary Section Unit, will Veritor & Tubbs, as these were not obtainable for the Ordnance (E.A. 4193)	(M)
			Forwarded application to H.Q. for Major Foyn & the appointed S.O.D.M.S.	(M)
			Rec'd from H.Q., copy of Opinion of Aulie Fore, asking for number of all unit [?] fit for overseas. V asking for immediate action. Forwarded same to all medical units.	(M)
			Rec'd copy of 3rd Army Memo re War Diary (3A/535/9)	(M)
			Forwarded hence to N.U. asking that early action might be taken re the issue of Orders to the Medical units, as great inconvenience is caused + uncertainty of officials of work, by the uncertainty to say others we are issued to this Office (E.A. 4200)	(M)
"	23rd/12/15		Received + circulated W.O. letter 24/San.No/4578 (A.G.1) 7 3.11.15 and C.F. letter (R. CF/1895(M)) 7 16.12.15. re Medical Ranks v fleeing of men in	(M)

Army Form C. 2118.

WAR DIARY
INTELLIGENCE SUMMARY
(Erase heading not required.)

Page 5

Place	Date	Hour	Summary of Events and Information	Remarks and references to Appendices
B. STAFFORD	Dec.			
Bishop Stortford	23rd.12.15		Various categories A.D.C.D.V.E.	
"	26th.12.15		Forwarded memo to Head Qrs regarding billeting accommodation in STAFFORD WALDEN	(X)
			for Men attending Course of Sanitary Duties.	(X)
"	27th.12.15		G.O.C. inspected 2/4 Field Ambulance. Was pleased with her Transport &c.	(X)
"	28th.12.15		Inspected all internal arrangements of 2/5 Field Ambulance, and	
			instructions re Scabies House & Cook house.	(X)
"	29th.12.15		Capt Sempton R.A.M.C. reported for duty. Posted him to R.E.	
"	30.12.15		heads for the application of R.B.C. baths. St Alban. The two Motor Ambulances	
			as 2 has been taken away & Promised Reynolds & renewal with repair.	(X)
			Memo to Head Quarters that Capt Carrick 97th Provisnl Field Ambulance	(X)
			be posted to 2/3. H.T. and 1st up to Form AF. Z.624.	
"	31st.12.15		W.O. Ltr ren_____ (9/Gen No 137 43 (S.D.2)) Authorizing inclusion in	
			returns of Officers & Field Ambulance &c.'s	(X)

E.J.Bowlbr
COLONEL
ASSISTANT DIRECTOR OF
MEDICAL SERVICES
60TH (LONDON) DIVISION.